GREAT DANES

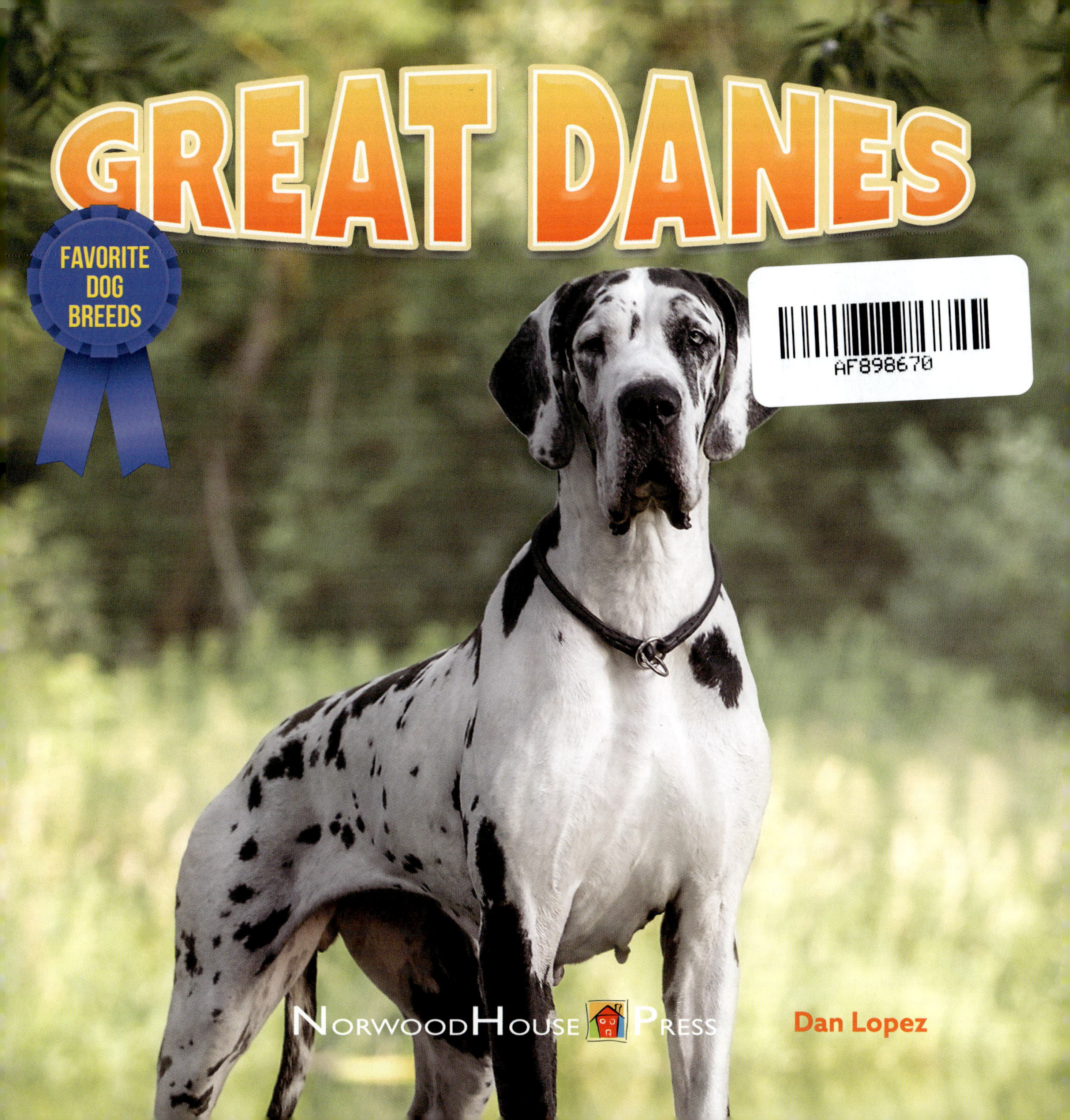

FAVORITE DOG BREEDS

NorwoodHouse Press

Dan Lopez

Cataloging-in-Publication Data

Names: Lopez, Dan.
Title: Great danes / Dan Lopez.
Description: Buffalo, NY : Norwood House Press, 2027. | Series: Favorite dog breeds | Includes glossary and index.
Identifiers: ISBN 9781978580329 (pbk.) | ISBN 9781978580336 (library bound) | ISBN 9781978580343 (ebook)
Subjects: LCSH: Great Dane--Juvenile literature. | Mastiff breeds--Juvenile literature.
Classification: LCC SF429.G7 L67 2027 | DDC 636.73--dc23

Published in 2027 by
Norwood House Press
2544 Clinton Street
Buffalo, NY 14224

Designer: Rhea Magaro
Editor: Tricia Hoffman

Photo credits: Cover, p.1 AI_Er/Shutterstock.com; p.4 Miroshnikova Arina/Shutterstock.com; p.5 Shutterstock AI; p.7 nik174/Shutterstock.com; p.8 WilleeCole Photography/Shutterstock.com; p.9 Wirestock Creators/Shutterstock.com; p.11 Guy J. Sagi/Shutterstock.com; p.12 Karin Jaehne/Shutterstock.com; p.14 lunamarina/Shutterstock.com; p.15 Olga Shusters/Shutterstock.com; p.16 Valmir Fernando/Shutterstock.com; p.19 TamaraLSanchez/Shutterstock.com; p.21 Dmussman/Shutterstock.com;

Printed in the United States of America

CPSIA compliance information: Batch #CSNHP27: For further information contact Norwood House Press at 1-800-237-9932.

TABLE OF CONTENTS

Meet the Great Dane

Great Danes are popular pets. Dogs of this **breed** are known for their large size. They are some of the tallest dogs in the world! Even though Great Danes are giants, they are **gentle**.

The cartoon character Scooby-Doo is a Great Dane.

What Do Great Danes Look Like?

From the ground to their shoulders, Great Danes can be 32 inches (82 centimeters) tall. When they stand on their hind legs, they are taller than most people!

Great Danes have massive heads with square jaws. Their ears can droop down or stand up straight.

They can weigh 175 pounds (79 kilograms). These dogs are huge, but their balance is good. They walk with a smooth, proud **gait**.

Great Danes have short, smooth, glossy **coats**. They can be black, white, **fawn**, or gray. Some have a black and white patchwork pattern.

Where Do Great Danes Come From?

People from the country of Denmark are called Danes. But Great Danes are not from Denmark. They were first bred in the country of Germany. No one is sure how they got their name.

Long ago, people used Great Danes to hunt for wild **boars**.

Do Great Danes Make Good Pets?

Great Danes are **easygoing** and friendly.

They are **affectionate** to people.

As long as they are trained not to play rough, these dogs are good with little kids. They make great family pets.

A Great Dane is alert and brave. It makes a good **watchdog**. A robber who sees this big dog will usually leave in a hurry!

What Do Great Danes Need?

Owning a Great Dane is a big **commitment**. These dogs need space to run and play. They need room to stretch out and sleep. They eat a lot of food, which can be expensive.

Great Danes are big and powerful, so they must have good behavior. Lessons help puppies learn how to act around people.

Glossary

affectionate (uh-FEK-shuh-nit): loving and caring

boars (borz): wild pigs with tusks

breed (breed): one type or kind of an animal

coats (kohts): the hair or fur that covers animals' bodies

commitment (kuh-MIT-muhnt): a promise to take care of something or be responsible for it

easygoing (ee-zee-GOH-ing): relaxed and carefree; not stressed out

fawn (fawn): a light brown color like the color of a young deer's coat

gait (gayt): a way of walking

gentle (JEN-tuhl): soft and mild; not rough

watchdog (WAHCH-dawg): a dog kept to guard property

Thinking Questions

1. What could you compare to the height of a Great Dane?

2. What colors can Great Danes be?

3. Where do Great Danes come from in the world?

4. Describe a Great Dane's personality.

5. Why is training important for Great Danes?

Index

About the Author

Dan Lopez is a writer who loves dogs! He has a German shepherd named Hans and an Irish setter named Tam. They love to go for walks in the woods together. Sometimes, they jump in the lake for a swim. Dan lives in Indiana with his wife and three kids.